TRIPLE PLAY!

Gay Sizemore Sauer

TRIPLE PLAY!

ReadersMagnet, LLC

Bullies Strike Out

This book is dedicated to four gentlemen who have
brightened my life: my husband, Ray Sauer, Sr.;
my son Ray Sauer, Jr. (Skip); my brother, Bill Sizemore,
Jr., and my son-in-law Kenny Kloss. These men represent
the best that all men should aspire to, and they have been
an abiding blessing to all who know and love them.

STORY 1
A REAL TEAM PLAYER

Buddy was very excited. He had been selected to try out for his community's baseball team. There would only be 20 boys playing on the team, and everyone he knew really wanted to make the team. He had been recommended by his coach at school. "I know you have what it takes to make the team," the coach said, "so give it your best shot."

The selection process would take about a week. On the first day, Buddy thought he counted at least thirty-five boys his age. It was kind of sad to think that fifteen of them would not make the team, and would have to settle for some other kind of summer activity.

One of the things the team's coaches had the boys do was run the bases. Buddy could run very fast, so this wasn't really a test, as far as he was concerned. However, as he ran past some of the competition, he noticed that some of the boys were having some problems. One boy especially caught his attention. This boy was a bit smaller than the others, and he had a strained look on his face. When the base running practice was over, he was seated on the ground near the boy and he asked, "Was that too tough for you?"

"No," the boy said, looking up into Buddy's face. "I just needed to use the bathroom real bad, so it proved harder than it should have been. After I got to the locker room and tended to that problem, I was okay."

"What's your name? I don't think I ever saw you at school. I'm called Buddy."

"My name is Benny. I didn't go to school here. Our family moved here in early spring, but I stayed behind with relatives to finish the school year in my old school."

The two boys continued to get acquainted during the break. Then everyone was told to head for the outfield to shag flies. Buddy noticed that Benny was running after the balls in a stumbling manner.

"What's the matter with your running now?"

"Several things. These are not my shoes, and they do not fit me at all. I think I have already developed a blister on my left foot. Some of my things are still at my aunt's house, including my shoes. I'll have to use these until mine get here."

Buddy continued to befriend Benny. The next day at practice he brought an extra pair of shoes of his own and had Benny try them. They fit better, and Benny had a better day.

The attention Buddy gave Benny did not go unnoticed. Some of Buddy's friends cornered him by the water fountain. "What are you doing, pal? You are being awful nice to that newcomer. Don't you know he's competing for the same position you are trying for on the team? He needs to be squashed like a bug right at the start. Don't let him get the notion that he's going to make this team."

Buddy looked at his friends with an awkward expression on his face. By now he had invested a lot of time in helping Benny, and it didn't occur to him that it might cost him a chance to play on the team because Benny would make the team at his, Buddy's, expense. However, he really liked Benny's attitude and willingness to accept good advice.

On the afternoon when the selections would be announced, one of the coaches took Buddy aside and spoke to him quietly. "We have noticed the kindness you have extended to Benny. It has helped that kid a lot. He has a fine arm and will make a fine ball player, and you can take some credit for that. What he really needed was someone to make him feel welcome, and you filled the bill perfectly."

Before Buddy could say anything, the coach continued, "What we coaches really want on this team are players who know how to help and encourage one another. Your own playing skills need a lot of work, but your teamwork is right on target, and you will be selected as one of the twenty because of that. So keep up the good work, Buddy."

CONGRATS

Buddy could hardly believe what he had just heard. Later after practice was over the names of those who made the team were posted on the locker room door. Buddy quickly located his name, and just above it appeared Benny's name! They had made the team. Among those fifteen who were disappointed were the friends that had urged Buddy to stop being friendly and helpful to Benny. Buddy had learned a valuable lesson: being nice and friendly, especially to newcomers, could make all the difference in your own success.

Benny became the team's winning pitcher, and right behind the plate guiding him through each inning, was his good friend Buddy, the team's catcher. They were the team's leaders, and the other eighteen players looked up to them with great respect. "Some games we win because we are good, but some of the close ones we win because we work as a team. Looking out for one another pays off," they all agreed.

STORY 2
A REAL KRACKER JACK

When the boy was quite young, his father tried to explain his unusual name. The explanation helped some but did not stop the teasing he put up with among the boys and girls in his new classroom at school.

Several generations ago in his family, a great-great-great grandparent immigrated to the United States from Poland. The immigration officer looking over the arrival's papers shook his head. "No one will ever spell or pronounce this name the way it should be. I see you are from Krakow, the capitol of Poland. Suppose we get rid of all those r-z-n-v-y combinations but keep the *K* at the beginning. Your name in the U.S. will be Krakor, kind of like the town in Poland you left. Easy enough to spell and pronounce. Believe me, you will thank me for it later." The immigrating family, with very limited English, understood only that they would have to change their name if they were to live happily in America. After that generation, the name *Krakor* became *Kracker,* which was even easier to pronounce.

In the first generation or two following, the family lived in Polish neighborhoods in big U.S. cities, and the name *Kracker* was no problem. In the fourth generation, however, an ambitious young Kracker moved to Texas to work. He had married a fine young woman, and before long they began their family. The first child was a boy, whom they named John Kracker, Jr. Since his father's name was John, and he had a cousin whose name was Johnny, the family called this son Jack, a familiar nickname used for John. (They knew this, because President John F. Kennedy had been nicknamed *Jack.*) Little Jack Kracker was a sturdy youngster, well behaved and always polite. He got along well with the children in his neighborhood. Then he started school and met an entire new population of boys and girls from other neighborhoods, and he learned something sad. Not all boys and girls had been taught to be kind and polite. They couldn't tease him because of his looks: he was blonde, blue-eyed, strong and athletic. They couldn't tease him because of his grades: he was bright, paid attention, and always made a straight-A report card. They made fun of him for the silliest of reasons: his name.

"He's a Crackerjack!" they yelled. "Yeah, popcorn in a box!"

Their rudeness made Jack even more shy, and he withdrew from those he had hoped to be friends with. This is the way things stood throughout elementary school. Jack Cracker never seemed to fit in with the other children. He poured himself into his schoolwork and tried to ignore the lonely times he spent on the playground.

Jack finally told his parents about the teasing, and they advised him to continue his polite behavior and not react to the rudeness. In sixth grade something unusual developed, and it changed things in a very positive way. The teacher gave the children a special assignment. They were to do some research on holiday customs in a foreign country, write a report on it, and demonstrate it for the other children in the class. Jack's mother had a remarkable idea!

Mrs. Kracker's people had come to the U.S. from England, so she decided to help Jack understand a favorite English custom—which, by the way, would incorporate his Polish last name (or the Americanized version of his Polish last name!). She took him on a shopping trip into Houston, the nearest big city, to visit a store which specialized in British imports. She showed him the boxes of 'crackers' which were popular table favors at holiday dinner parties. The manager of the store was happy to show Jack how the cracker worked. It was a short cardboard tube filled with candy and small toys, wrapped in holiday paper and had a device in each end that, when the ends were pulled, produced a "pop". Out poured the candy and the little gifts, and Jack laughed out loud. He had laughed so little this year that his mother was overjoyed. They bought several boxes of the 'cracker' favors, and went home to do the research.

CHRISTMAS

CHRISTMAS
CRACKERS

When the day came for Jack to give his report, he surprised his classmates by standing in front of the class and announcing that his research had been about 'crackers'. He ignored their giggles and smirks, and went on to explain the great festive dinner parties the British were famous for. Then he reached into the bag at his feet and pulled out one of the crackers to show them what he was talking about. He pulled the ends, producing the popping sound, and not a few of his classmates squealed in perfect delight, especially when they saw the candy fall from it. He further made them happy when he proceeded to pass a cracker to each of them. He concluded his report by saying to his classmates, "Merry Christmas, all of you. May you have a cracking good time this holiday season."

He heard some of those who had teased him say, "Wow, he's a real Cracker Jack, isn't he?" The remark was not said rudely, but in admiration.

Jack's good humor and his ability to laugh *with* his tormenters about his name accomplished more than all the good manners and good grades and polite behavior did. They realized that their tall, blonde, blue-eyed classmate was a real sport, and teasing him was a waste of time. In fact, they decided that he should be invited to play on their team. This he did, and from that time forward, Jack Cracker was not only the most polite and brightest student in the school, but he became its athletic star as well.

As the students grew out of their silly immaturity, they decided that Jack Cracker was the kind of boy they most wanted to be like. Before long they couldn't remember that they had ever been rude or unkind. But Jack remembered. He used his experience to be kinder than ever to any new kid who entered the school. He knew how important it was to be a friend to them. His behavior did not go unnoticed, and before long the attitude and atmosphere of the school changed from one of indifference and bullying to one of good manners and kindness. The children were all little cracker jacks at making friends with newcomers.

Some reading this story might label it a 'fable.' If you are one, try Jack Kracker's solution—be a friend to *everyone*, even those who mistreat you. You might be surprised at the miracle you are able to create.

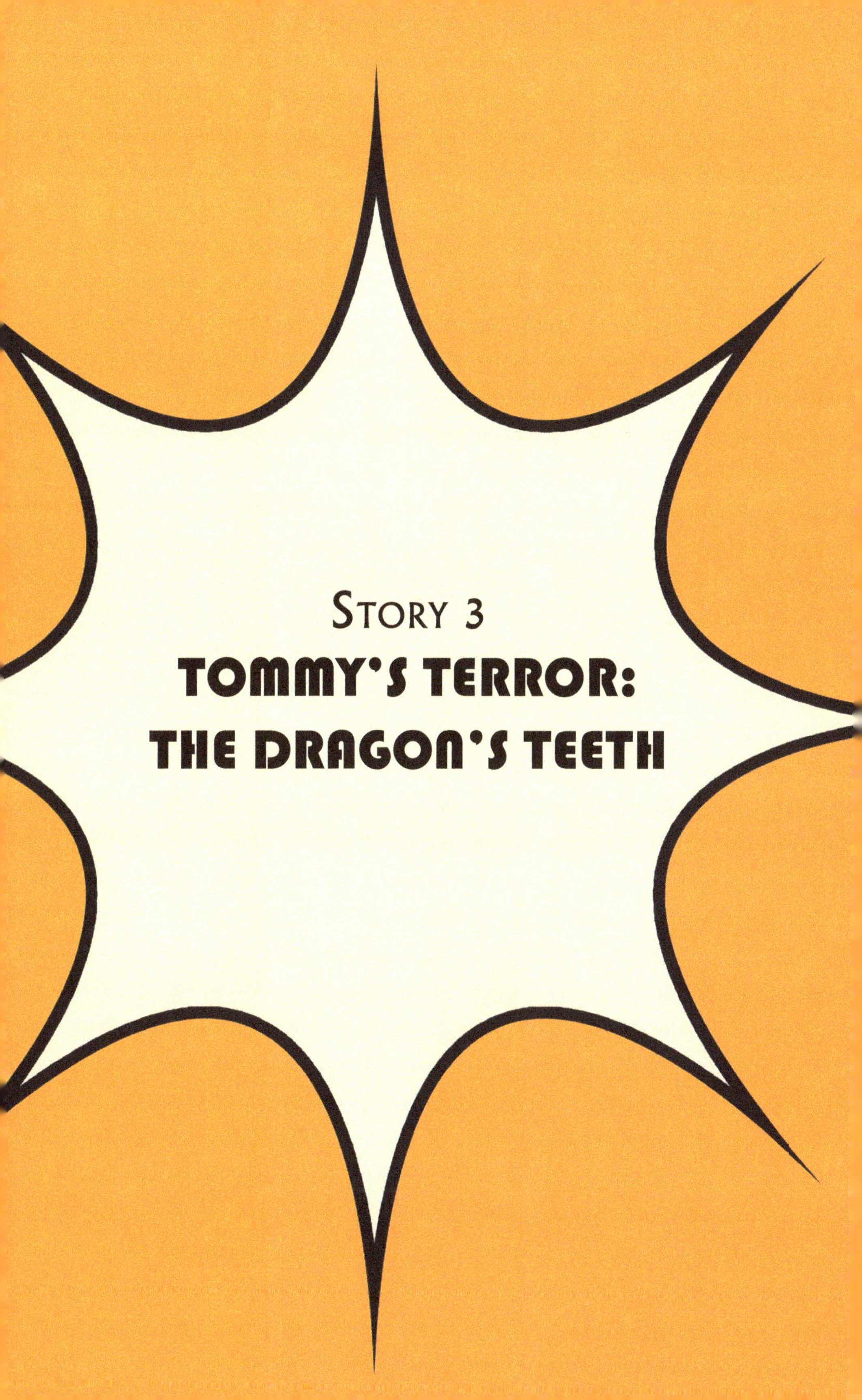
STORY 3

TOMMY'S TERROR:
THE DRAGON'S TEETH

Tommy was nine years old, and he knew he was a big boy who could hold his own in any fight. He was bigger, in fact, than most of the boys in his class. He was known to laugh at other kids his age who showed they were afraid of one thing or another.

"What sissies!" Tommy would shout. "Where's their courage?"

Tommy was not afraid to wade into any fight, and he explained to any adult who came to break it up that he was just trying to help 'the little guy.' That was a lie, of course, because he only wanted to fight, to be a bully.

His classmates knew that Tommy just liked to show off his ability to win any fight. The children were mostly afraid of Tommy, and gave him a wide berth when they met him coming down the hall. Obviously, Tommy hadn't made many friends in school or in his neighborhood. This did not seem to bother Tommy. He actually enjoyed his role of being the school's bully.

More than once Tommy's parents had been called by the school to come in and discuss Tommy's anti-social behavior with the principal and the teachers. For those who do not know what 'anti-social' means, it describes people like Tommy who do not get along well with others and do things to break up the social harmony of the group. Not a pretty description of a nine-year-old boy, but it really did describe Tommy.

"Oh, he'll grow out of it," Tommy's father said. "I was pretty tough at that age myself."

"Of course he will," added Tommy's mother. "After all, boys will be boys."

This attitude, of course, only encouraged Tommy to continue being a bully and calling everyone else a sissy. His teachers threw up their hands in despair and wondered what would ever become of Tommy.

This unhappy situation might have gone on for many years except that something very dramatic happened to Tommy following the Halloween celebration the year when he was about to become ten years old.

Tommy had gone out trick-or-treating, accompanied by his mother, whom he tried to run away from. "Who needs a mother making the rounds with them—sissies, that's who."

After several hours of making all the houses in the neighborhood, Tommy returned home and went to his room. He took with him his pillow case filled with all kinds of candy. His mother reminded him to eat only a piece or two, and save the rest for the days ahead. Tommy ignored her. He was very good at ignoring whatever adults said to him. His attitude was, "What do they know?"

Tommy picked around at the candy in the sack and found some pieces that he really liked. He gobbled these down first. Then he ate several other pieces that were also good and chewy. His mother called from the living room to remind him that it was late and he should get to bed. Tomorrow was a very busy day, she added, reminding him of his dental appointment.

Tommy paid little attention, but he was getting tired, so he went into his bathroom to brush his teeth. He laughed to see the traces of chocolate appear on them. He laughed again when he watched the chocolate-colored water go down the drain after he rinsed his mouth.

"That's cool!" the boy said. "I look like a real monster!"

Tommy went to bed, but not before carefully placing the pillow sack full of candy beside the bed pillow on which he finally laid down his head. As he lay there thinking about all the sights and sounds of his Halloween Trick or Treating, he continually reached into the bag and unwrapped one piece of candy after another. He threw the wrappers on the floor.

Tommy was very tired: he had covered a lot of territory that evening in search for more and more candy. He was also feeling very unsettled in his stomach. It did not occur to him that the enormous amount of candy he had eaten had anything to do with this.

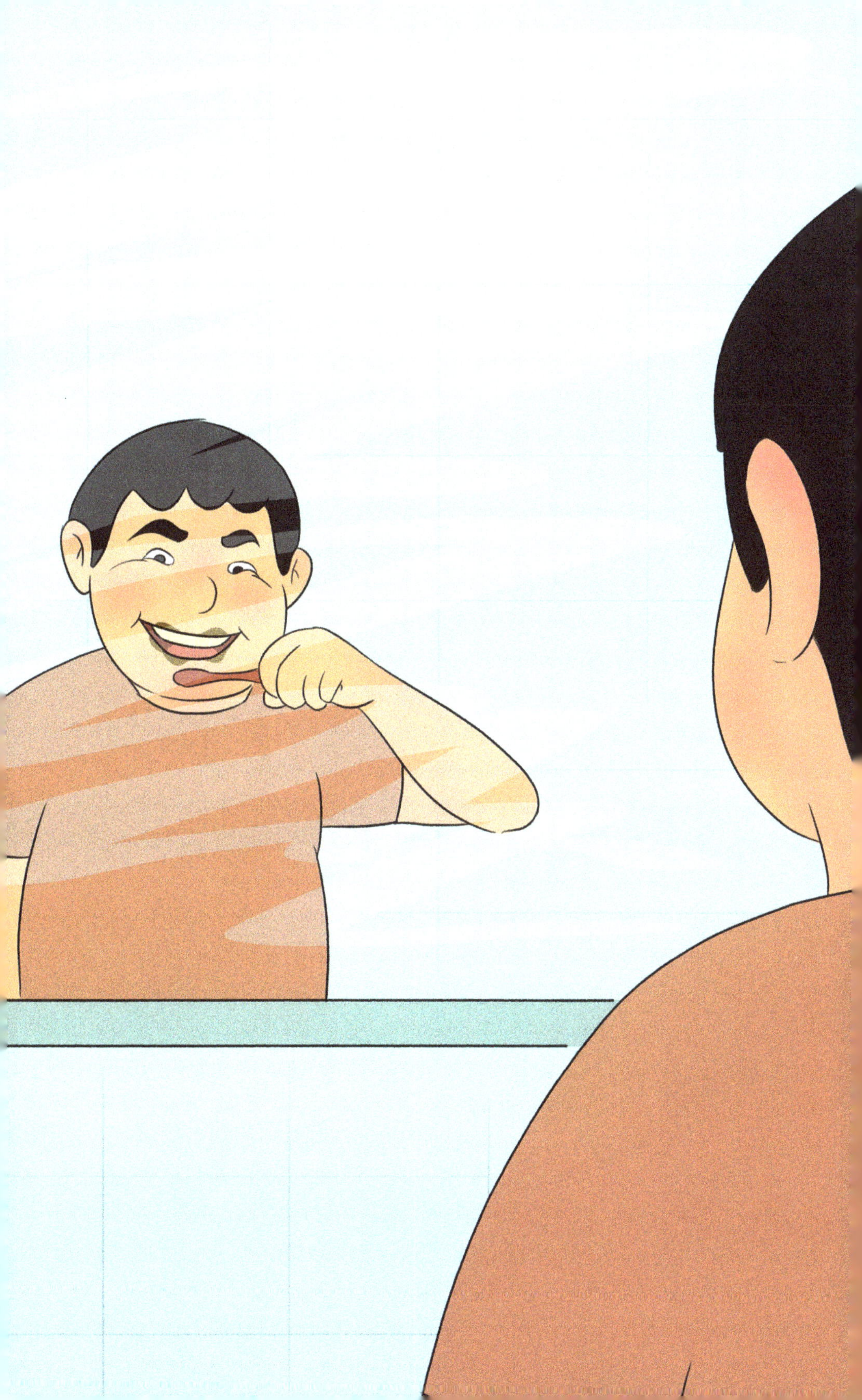

At just about the time he was nodding off to sleep, he heard a frightening noise outside his bedroom window. Then he saw an enormous shape appear which seemed to resemble a dragon.

"This can't be real—dragons are just in comic books!" Tommy said, but his eyes were wide open and he could feel the hair on his head prickle and begin to rise. "It's just not real!" he repeated in shocked protest.

The dragon apparently hadn't heard Tommy, because it forced open the window and began to wiggle his awful form through the window frame. The dragon was very scaly, and it was colored in the most awful shades of green, yellow, and brown. Putrid colors.

Tommy grabbed the pillow case of candy to cover his face, because he couldn't stand to see that awful form that was now in his own bedroom. He could feel the heat that came from the beast, and as he peeked around the candy pillow case, he could see fire coming from the dragon's mouth. The fire was bad, and it smelled awful, but it was the teeth that really terrified Tommy. Those teeth could be used to gobble him alive.

In fact, that was what the dragon was saying to Tommy between belches of fire: "I want to eat you in great bites—the way you gobbled down all that candy. I also like Trick or Treating, and the trick is, you are going to be my treat!" This awful comment was followed by a great belch of fire. The yellow teeth of the dragon sparkled and lit up as if a switch had turned them on.

Tommy struggled to scream out in terror, but his voice was frozen. Then the light in his room turned on and his mother appeared. "What's wrong, dear?" she asked.

Tommy couldn't answer. He kept looking at the window where he had seen the terrible dragon with the yellow teeth belching fire and threatening to eat him alive. He looked up helplessly at his mother.

"You must have had a bad dream, Tommy. Now go back to sleep."

Tommy tried, but he kept staring at the window. After a while, the dragon reappeared and said, "You're not so tough after all. There are many things bigger and tougher than you. How about forgetting about fighting everybody and instead getting along with them? Then no big horrible thing like myself will come along and threaten to eat you alive."

Tommy promised to change his ways. The dragon belched out a few more flames and bared his big yellow teeth, then, mercifully, he left the room.

Before long—it seemed only a few minutes—Tommy's mother entered the room again.

"You must get up, Tommy. Get those teeth brushed and put on these clothes I've laid out for you. Today's very important. You have a dental appointment, remember? Be sure to brush your teeth well; they must be nice and clean so the dentist can examine them."

Tommy was unable to say anything, but he did go into his bathroom and he took a good look at his chocolate-smeared teeth. He grabbed his toothbrush and began to erase all the evidence of a frightful night he wanted to forget completely. He especially wanted to forget the dreadful sight of the dragon's teeth.

Tommy didn't forget the dragon's warning, however, to change his ways.

No one in the school, not his parents, not anyone who knew Tommy ever understood what had come over him. But he was a completely different boy after Halloween, and by the time Christmas came around, no one even remembered that he had ever been accused of being the school's bully. But Tommy knew what had happened: those dragon teeth would scare the bully out of anyone! And in January he made a Resolution never to be the bully he once had been.

10620 Treena Street, Suite 230

San Diego, California,

CA 92131 USA

www.readersmagnet.com

1.619.354.2643

Copyright 2019 All Rights Reserved

Printed in the USA
CPSIA information can be obtained
at www.ICGtesting.com
LVHW060850050224
770951LV00007B/30